God's Blessings on you always.

In Jesus Love
Sister Regina Marie

COLLECTION OF POETRY ABOUT
SAINT FRANCIS OF ASSISI

TWO PRAYERS FOR TWO STONES

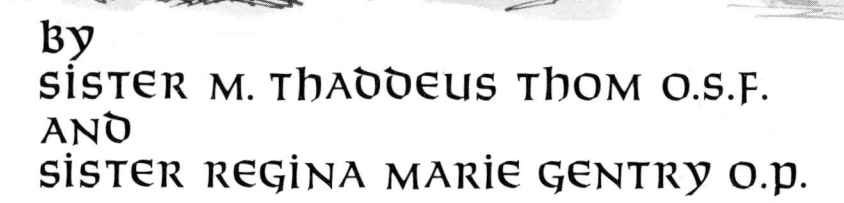

by
SISTER M. THADDEUS THOM O.S.F.
AND
SISTER REGINA MARIE GENTRY O.P.

FRANCISCAN HERALD PRESS
Chicago, Illinois 60609

Two Prayers for Two Stones by Sister M. Thaddeus Thom O.S.F. and Sister Regina Marie Gentry O.P., copyright © 1976 by Franciscan Herald Press. All reprint permissions of poetry or art reserved to the publisher.

Library of Congress Cataloging in Publication Data

Thom, Thaddeus.
  Two prayers for two stones.
    1. Francesco d'Assisi, Saint, 1182-1226—Poetry. I. Gentry, Regina Marie, joint author. II. Title. PS3570.H48T9   811'.5'4   76-18239
ISBN 0-8199-0616-6

MADE IN THE UNITED STATES OF AMERICA

FOREWORD

I have written poetry ever since I can remember—or, at least,—I called it poetry. When the thought of writing a whole book of poems about the life of St. Francis crossed my mind two years ago, I thought it was just that—something that had crossed my mind. But, when I expressed this thought to Mother M. Viola, who had always been most encouraging about my smaller writings, she urged me to develop the idea. Now, I hoped for a collaborator, someone to share with, to become enriched by, and hopefully, to enrich. Then it happened in the providence of God. I paid an unanticipated visit to the Perpetual Rosary Monastery and asked for one of the nuns whom I knew. She was not available. However, Sister Regina Marie was. During the course of our conversation, we began discussing poetry and to my surprise, Sister had been a Franciscan for a number of years until their community merged with another and Sister desired a less active form of life. Thus she joined this Dominican group in Syracuse, New York. She had written some poetry about St. Francis, some of which she has set to music, and she was willing to share it with me. From that point on we met at intervals, to share, to discuss and to enjoy. I neglected to mention that Sister Regina Marie is blind. Perfect, I thought, she can see things I will never be able to see, and she has!

We would like to express our gratitude to the members of our communities who have encouraged us in this work: our major superiors; Mother M. Viola, O.S.F. and Mother M. Paul, O.P.; Sister Tarcisia, O.S.F., for her patience in proofreading and analyzing for authenticity; Sister M. Josella, O.S.F. and Sister Francis Agnes, O.S.F. who contributed to the effectiveness of our poetic attempt at interpreting the life of St. Francis with their fascinating sketches.

This has been a marvelous experience for us. We hope you, too, will find it stimulating and rewarding.

Sister M. Thaddeus Thom, O.S.F.

To
Mother M. Viola, O.S.F.,
whose love for
all things Franciscan
has been the
turning point
in my life and
the essence of
our community.

CONTENTS

Foreword	III	
Troubadors of God	3	Illustration
Free Spirit	4	Illustration
Protector	6	Illustration
His Early Blindness	9	
The Dye-ing Cellar	11	
Shafts of Light	13	Illustration
Two Prayers for Two Stones	15	Illustration
Conversion	17	
Time-ness	19	
Solitude	20	
Carceri	21	
A Time of Locusts and Honey	23	Illustration
Ultimate Reality	24	
The Rule of Life	26	
Saint Mary of the Angels	28	Illustration
Pax et Bonum	30	Illustration
Values	32	
Brother Juniper and the Pig	34	
Brother Juniper and the See-Saw	38	
Brother Fly	40	
La Verna	43	Illustration
The Blindness of St. Francis	44	
Be Gentle, Brother Fire	45	
The Lost Rule	46	
Hymn to Saint Clare	48	Illustration
The Heavenly Song	50	
The Eternal Gaze	51	Illustration
Watchman	53	
These Friendships Were Made in Heaven	54	
Francis Blesses Assisi	55	Illustration
Canticle to Brother Francis	57	

ABOUT THE POETS

Sister M. Thaddeus Thom, OSF, is a member of the Third Franciscan Order of Syracuse, New York, and is presently engaged in teaching at the Assumption Academy where she is the Senior Advisor, Yearbook Moderator, Chairperson of the English Department and Advisor to the Junior Third Order. Sister lives at the Portiuncula Hermitage in Fayetteville, NY, which she has directed for the past three years. On weekends and during vacations Sister makes retreat facilities available to members of her community and other Sisters in the area. Many of her poems, book reviews, and articles have appeared in various periodicals. Sister holds a BA in English from LeMoyne College in Syracuse, NY, an MA in English from Catholic University in Washington, DC and is an MA candidate in Franciscan Studies at St. Bonaventure University in Olean. Sister is a member of the National League of American Pen Women.

Sister Regina Marie Gentry, OP, is a member of the Perpetual Rosary Monastery of Dominican nuns in Syracuse, NY. Sister has been at this monastery for eight years. Previous to that time, Sister was a member of a Franciscan community, but at the time of its merger with another more active group, Sister transferred to this contemplative community. Although Sister has been blind since birth, she is an able musician and poet as well as the moderator of the Secular Dominican Third Order. BS in social studies; main education and LL.B from Seton Hall, New Jersey.

ABOUT THE ARTISTS

Sister M. Joselle Orlando, OSF, is a member of the Third Franciscan Order of Syracuse, NY, and is presently Art instructor at the Assumption Academy. Sister is also Junior Class Advisor and moderator of the National Honor Society. Her vocal and musical gifts are used in directing the mixed chorus at the Assumption Academy. AA from Maria Regina College; BFA from Syracuse University.

Sister Francis Agnes Ryan, OSF, is a member of the Third Franciscan Order of Syracuse, NY, and is presently Art instructor at Bishop Ludden High School in Syracuse, NY. She holds a BS degree from LeMoyne College; an MFA from the University of Notre Dame and is also a candidate for an MA in Franciscan Studies at St. Bonaventure University in Olean. Sister is a member of the N.Y.S. Art Teachers' Association and acts as chairperson of the Advisory Committee for the National Scholastic Art Awards Program in the Syracuse area.

TWO PRAYERS FOR TWO STONES

Poetry by:
Sister M. Thaddeus Thom, OSF
Sister Regina Marie Gentry, OP

Illustrations by:
Sister M. Joselle Orlando, OSF
Sister Francis Agnes Ryan, OSF

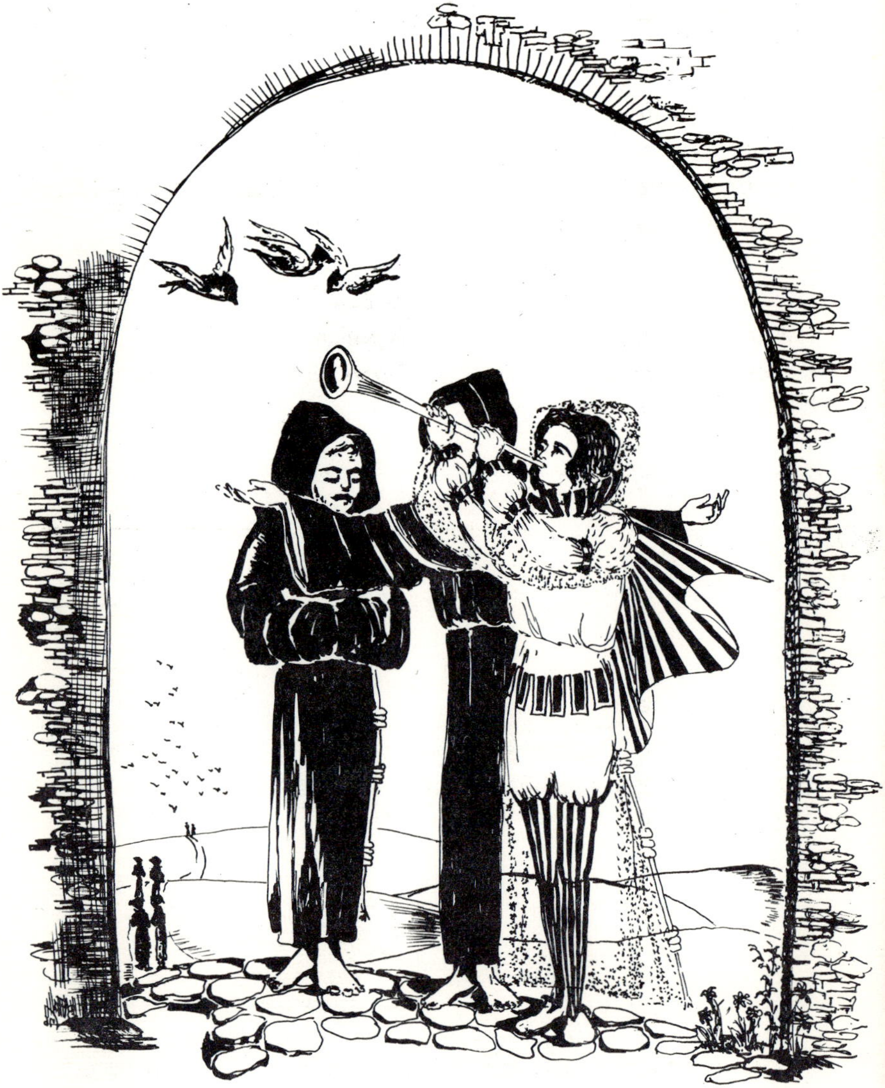

TROUBADORS OF GOD

We are troubadors of God, with the larks our spirits fly,
Soaring with our songs of love to the grandeur of the sky.
Father Francis, fill our souls with your music clear and sweet
That the praise you sang so well all your children may repeat.

We are heralds of the King, as our Father was of yore;
With all creatures we unite in His praise forever more.
Francis, make our voice resound over all the din of hell;
Put your song upon our lips as the praise of God we tell.

We are minstrels of the Queen, tender melodies we sing;
Bliss unspeakable it is, loving gifts of song to bring.
Singer of the Umbrian hills! Knight of Mary, brave and strong,
We, your fervent tribute join with our ceaseless joyful song.

We are followers of Christ on the road to Calv'ry steep;
At our Father's wounds we gaze; in our hearts Christ's wounds
    we keep.
Servants of the Crucified, sin and hatred we destroy.
Francis, make us sing and live your own true and perfect joy!

(This poem was inspired by the free troubador spirit Francis experienced in his youth, which developed into his love for all creation—the last stanza is a plea for all Franciscans to follow.   Sr. R.M.)

FREE SPIRIT

Francis—
*   friendly, free and fair,*
Fancied living anywhere.

No worldly problems held him down,
The care-free boy of Assisi town.

Good, loving, valiant, too,
War, battle—he would pursue.

Glory, victory, honors won;
These the desires of Bernardone's son.

Armed and armored off he sped
Like any Assisi lad well-bred.

His father proudly hailed his son
As if sending him for a day of fun.

Even in war—a generous lad,
Giving his armor to one poorly clad,

Recognizing at his tender age
The reverence due an experienced sage.

Unknown to Francis or his kin
His greatest enemy lay within.

A fever struck before he arrived
At the battle fields where he hoped to thrive.

The call—so plain to us in the present—
Made him, at his return, an unwelcome peasant.

(Francis, a delicate youth, was always a dreamer. His father, too, entertained dreams for him—so as Francis went off to war, his father clothed him royally—neither one dreamed of God's intervention nor of Francis' illness and embarrassing return to Assisi without honors.   Sr. M.T.)

PROTECTOR

The great citadel stands proudly high,
Piercing clouds and darkened sky.
Below, the town rests in peace and sleep
Knowing the citadel will vigil keep.

Yet—in one house of the little town
A young man long and late knelt down.
  His face is strained; his eyes are closed;
  His manner tense, to prayer disposed.

Were war and illness too much for him?
He regards himself as a man of sin!
  Where before he would dance, and joke and play,
  He avoids the places and people to pray.

His eyes are wet; his sighs profound;
Once, the King of Merriment he was crowned!
  His hands clasped tightly to his breast,
  In battle he wore Assisi's crest.

Strange battlefield, this tiny room;
More devastating than a cannons boom.
  Strange weapons—folded hands and sighs,
  Piercing even these darkened skies.

A night-long battle—till day breaks
And Assisi, from her repose awakes.
  The citadel yawns and closes its eyes
  To sunshine, flowers and bright-blue skies.

And in that very simple room—
Rising as if from his own tomb—
  Francis began another day,
  In his soul he'll hear Christ say:

"Is it better to serve the servant or Lord?"
And Francis will answer of his own accord.
"Thus, serve me, Francis, do My will—
Cease to play with ways that kill."

The citadel watches the drama below,
As night after night Francis struggles so,
While he shakes off the garb of pomp and pride
To embrace Lady Poverty as his Bride.

(Overlooking Assisi is a major fortress which had been a protection for the people of the town in earlier times and still stood proudly in Francis' day. Once Francis overcomes himself, he is no longer in need of physical protection.   Sr. M.T.)

His Early Blindness

Dame Pleasure closed your eyes to higher things;
You led your youth on gay adventure's wings;
Fine clothes, pretty girls, a kingly crown;
You had the money, so the wine went round.

Once came into your shop with outstretched palms
A beggar who would ask from you an alms;
You threw a coin to—just get rid of him;
Your pleasure-loving eyes were truly dim.

But with that gesture came an insight strange;
Something inside you made you want to change;
God's grace did spread upon those eyes of clay;
He bade you wash in the pool of Siloe.

Once, riding on your horse there came to view
A sight which was a bitter thing for you—
A leper! O what stench! You wished to run,
But no! You could not! What then must be done?

Within you heard a whisper: "Follow me!"
Down from your horse, you fell upon your knee;
Rising, you clasped the leper with a kiss;
Behold! What ecstasy! Behold! What bliss!

Then sweetness filled your being through and through;
Christ crucified now wholly mastered you;
"What you have done, you did it unto Me!"
"Praise be my Lord and thanks, for now I see!"

(Francis always enjoyed life and good times with others. Since he was educated along fine lines anything dirty or crude would be distasteful to him—hence the poor man or the leper would be loathsome to him. God enlightened his generous heart and gave him the gift of Himself.   Sr.R.M.)

THE DYE-ING CELLAR

Never before had he ventured below;
  He knew it was there.
Now—step by step—he smelled the heat;
  Step by step the stench increased.
Colors—draped—dripping;
  Colors flashing in the firelight—
Distorted by tears in his eyes;
  Distorted by persons colored
By his father's design.

No smile greeted him.
  No hand reached out even for an alms.
Eyes aflame with reflection;
  Stolid expressions watched him.
Hands raw with wet dye
  Wrung new cloths colored silently.
Only flames crackled.
  No human sound could be heard
Save the heavy breath of an old man,
  Multi-colored from years of work.

Young people, too, carried buckets,
  But, no laughter—no contentment—
Just necessary labor.
  "Oh, God, no! Human price is too great!"
His knees felt the moisture as he fell;
  Tears ran rivulets onto his chest.
"Somehow, they, too, must know the Gospel."

Into the bright air he led them;
  Like a piper he led them on.
Though they thought it strange—
  Was this not the owner's son?
Bright light offended eyes used to firelight.
  Warm air lifted spirits mildewed by dye.
"God wants men to see his creation."

Too soon the time is over.
  Francis rejoices in giving joy!
He rushes to share it with his father.
  No joy is there—only anger!
Deep discontent and frustration lash out
  To give Francis his reward for loving God.

The dye-ing cellar remains;
  Machine-like men remember that day
As cloth is dyed and dried,
  And a spark of hope is in their hearts—
"Perhaps there is a God who cares for us?"

(Francis' father was a cloth merchant and as such *probably* had a cellar for dyeing cloth. In this cellar, laborers worked for years without ever seeing daylight or smelling the freshness of the air since they began work before sunrise and finished after sunset. Francis tried to change this.   Sr.M.T.)

SHAFTS OF LIGHT

Before the cross the young man knelt—
No stranger to the gift of prayer—for—
From his youth he had been taught
By a tender Mother, ever fair.

*The flickering lamp sent shafts of light
Which caught his ever-curious gaze;
Through cracking walls and beams, alike,
Piercing like a sword of grace.
He knew not how, nor did he care
How he had wandered to this Church.
Within? Without? A voice he heard;
A deeper call to increase his search.*

*A builder now, he had become—
A mason for the work of God!
A gatherer of bricks and stone
A follower of the Christ-man's rod.*

*The prayer he prayed was old, indeed,
A prayer that many men might know.
The task, however, was quite new—
God, Himself, would have to show—
For was He not the Master-Builder!
A corner stone His Son had been—
And, he rich soul, must learn the way
To plot the journey for other men.*

(This poem is a fuller experience of Francis' response to Christ's command to "Repair My church!"   Sr. M.T.)

TWO PRAYERS FOR TWO STONES

"Two prayers for two stones,"
Cried the son of Peter Bernardone.
"One prayer for just one stone,"
He called as he walked alone.

"St. Damien's is sadly in need of repair—
Aren't there any townsfolk who really care?
The poor priest has only rags to wear
And the Lord's altar is quite bare."

"I promise two prayers for two stones,"
But the pilgrim continued his task alone.
Faces watching were shocked to see a Bernardone
Quite ragged, weather-worn and wind-blown.

A few children came out to see
The beggar—and were filled with glee
To cast a few stones to answer his plea
Then, turn fast and quickly flee.

"A prayer for a stone," he continued to implore.
The Lord above heard and sent him a corps
Of young men to help him restore
This Church of Damien—blessed forevermore.

(The Church of San Damiano lies outside the walls of Assisi. As Francis wandered about he happened upon this Church and upon entering was confronted with an icon of the crucified. Interiorly Christ asked Francis to repair His church. Francis, taking this command literally, began repairing San Damiano by begging stones from the townspeople.   Sr.M.T.)

CONVERSION

*Francis wondered as he fled life
in the city and the shop
if he was self-deluded
but—Christ's love put a stop
to his fantasy and revel
so—Christ's love must set him free—
free to seek a Gospel-living—
free in blessed poverty.*

*Darkened chambers only pointed to
a solitary path.
Contradicting worldly-wisdom led to
foolish saintliness.*

*Renunciation of all matters
held so dear by mortal men
gained an insight into riches
far beyond our human ken.*

*Hands which built with stone
those Churches
falling utterly to ruin
gleamed the brilliance of the Crucified
in His holy Easter tomb.*

*Leaving persons dearly loved
to serve Immortal Love alone,
Francis gained countless followers
he would never have sought at home.*

*Fighting devils whose chief glory
is to subject man to lust—
Francis' disciplined example brought him
the Poor Ladies' greatest trust.*

(This poem attempts to include all the aspects of Francis' conversion up to the establishment of the Second Order, then known as the Poor Ladies.   (Sr. M.T.)

TIME-NESS

For a time—
The soul wanders restlessly;
Wrestling with God's attraction.

Impossible!—it feels so drawn—
Almost sickened with desire;
Unable to contemplate God;
Unable to tolerate men!

Unhinged—disjointed—torn asunder
By Divine cloudiness;
Obscuring simple tasks—yet—
Never unmasking the Divine.

If only the soul could reach beyond.
If only it could penetrate this sublime curtain.

It asks in its agony—"Why? Who? How?

Only say it!—and it will be done!

Free me from this torment of love!"

(An attempt to describe the struggle of the interior man as he reaches out to the Unknown.   Sr. M.T.)

SOLITUDE

At last—alone with only bare stone,
And—no one to seek me out!

No one to heed my cries
Or aid me if I should shout.

A little space in time is all I asked—
Precious, alone-moments with God.

To struggle with a holy call—
Divine Love for this earthly clod.

An immersion on heavenly terms
In the treasures hidden for man to find.

A little space—a little place—
Infinite Love in the God-man's mind.

(Francis often went into solitude, after the example of Christ, the better to know his God.   Sr. M.T.)

CARCERI

Unity of opposites in nature—
Francis' life style.
Going to the heights to
    reach the depths—
Mounting high to become low—
Seeking the world-view
The better to see oneself.

(The word "carceri" means little cells. On Mt. Subasio there were many such natural cells formed of rock where Francis and his first followers went to pray to the Father in secret.   Sr. M.T.)

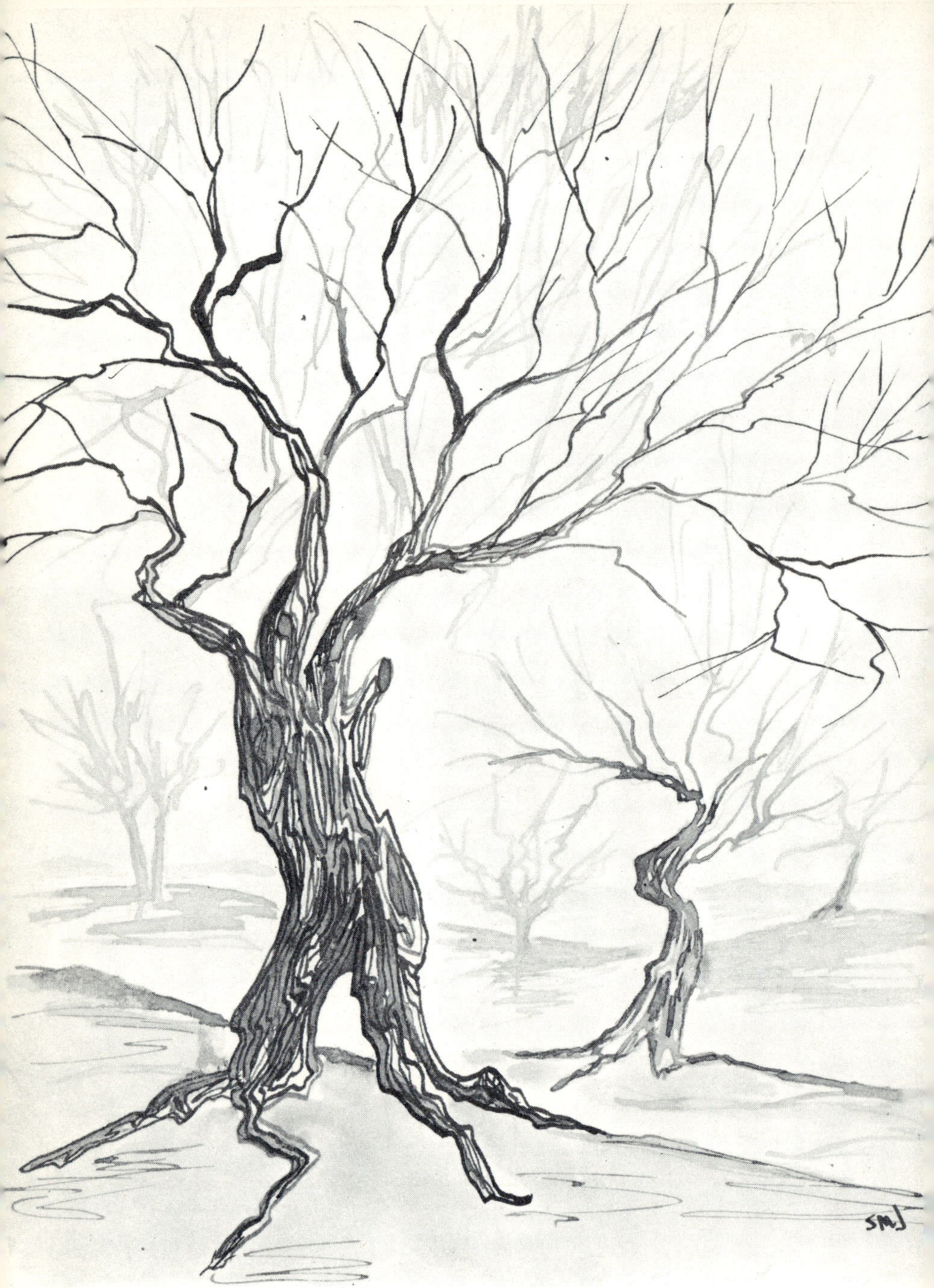
SMJ

A Time of Locusts and Honey

In the vagueness of our being
A hollow groaning breathes
Satisfaction from the Un-named
Which has been tasted.

Drenched with a new honey,
Its pleasantness seems to mock
The fulness of desire;
Life appears intrinsically new.

Puny knowledge! Which only estranges
Here . . . from . . . There . . . .

Human attempts
        labeled
                prayer!

(The special call to contemplation which was given to Francis seems like John the Baptist's locust and honey time in preparation for his work as precursor. A wild—yet sweet time of life.   Sr. M.T.)

ULTIMATE

My Most Beloved—
how can I hope to understand your Love—
no strength of mine; no knowledge of mine—
has led You to me.

Flames, higher than mind can surmise,
scorch my soul;
cleansing there—(what needs to be cleansed)
showing plainly that which is concealed.

How can I say what You are!
Distinguish Your Love—
separate It from mine!

Once apart—now joined
by an inescapable power—
yearning for return;
enraptured.

REALiTy

*Ascend—like blessed incense
to the very seat of His heights
and create a new journey
for a prodigal soul.*

*You tease me too much—
yet—I am here—where You will.*

*In life's tasks Your Spirit
overpowers my actions—
and—I wait—*
              upon Your Love.

(An attempt to explain the ultimate in acknowledging God as one's life; to give oneself over entirely to His will. Sr.M.T.)

THE RULE OF LIFE

"Scriptures, scriptures, I would see—
Open up a life for me.
A world that only my soul may see;
A world in love with poverty."

DENY THYSELF; TAKE UP THY CROSS;
CONSIDER ALL THE WORLD A LOSS.

"This I want, this I seek, this I desire—
My whole being is on fire!
This Rule shall be the life for those
Who follow in these humble clothes.

"Thrice-knotted cord, the three vows will inspire;
Tau cloth—the cross or martyr's choir.
The tonsured head—a preacher's mark;
To kindle a little apostolic spark.

*"And through the world we'll travel on
Paths that other men have gone—
But all in peace and joy and love,
Giving witness to the Lord above.*

*"No place our own—no things to gather;
No man or woman would we rather
Spend our time with than the poor—
Or—battle wits with the heathen Moor.*

*"Thus, we in faith, shall roam the earth
Until the time of our eternal birth."*

(In the little Church of San Nicolo, Francis and his first two followers sought a rule of life based on Gospel texts which were found by opening the Gospels three times at random.   Sr. M.T.)

SAINT MARY OF

St. Mary of the Angels, that tiny spot of earth
Where Francis gave his Order birth;
O blessed Portiuncula, enriched by God above,
From whence the world has gathered the fruits of Francis' love.

St. Mary of the Angels! Our Mother's favored spot;
This little wayside chapel can never be forgot!
O treasured "little Portion"—we thank God for this place;
Forth from its sacred precincts come benefits of grace.

St. Mary of the Angels! Look down, our Mother dear;
Keep in thy kindly patronage this little chapel here.
St. Mary of the Angels! How often do we kneel
To talk with you and Jesus, our secrets to reveal.

In Jesus' holy Presence, with thee our cause to plead,
St. Mary of the Angels, our Mother kind, indeed;
St. Mary of the Angels, thy loving care we claim
When in our convent chapel we softly breathe thy name.

※

(Portiuncula means "little portion" and is, indeed, a tiny chapel, where, as the story goes, angels visited. This deserted chapel was given to St. Francis and his first Friars by the Benedictines. However, Francis refused to accept ownership of any property and each year the Friars paid rent for its use by a basket of fish. It was here that the Order really had its beginnings and it was here that Francis died.   Sr. R.M.)

THE ANGELS

PAX ET BONUM

When Francis on love's missions went
  For all he chanced to meet,
His thoughtful tenderness he showed
  And warmly he did greet:
"Pax et bonum! Pax et bonum!"
  From his heart he'd say,
And thus, with wondrous joy and cheer
  He sent them on their way.

It is a welcome warm and deep,
  A verbal kiss of peace,
A cordial wish for all good things,
  That love for God increase:
"Pax et bonum! Pax et bonum!"
  Now we still repeat
The loving wish our Father made
  When we our brethren greet.

How good it is where brethren dwell
  In union's sweet accord,
And breathe for one another still
  This prayer unto our Lord:
"Pax et bonum! Pax et bonum!"
  Joyful notes resound,
And with this heartfelt tender wish
  May blessings great abound.

(Peace and all good things—was a favorite greeting of St. Francis and he wished his friars to greet all they met with this greeting.   Sr. R.M.)

VALUES ✳

Under the shadow of the sky and night
   where stars dance bravely on
   in this man's paradise proclaimed—
   no eyes the splendor watch;
   just sleep—or some may dream,
   but waking vision
   only dulls the nightly reality responses
   to a blessed moment flashing by.

Even those whom the splendid moment
   has re-possessed, stand idly spouting
   memorized textual conditions.

And in the heart of one man, claimed by God,
   a shadow folds the pages of a life
   tremblingly lived without gloss, without glass,
              without gloss.

One blessed moment flashing by.

His minor essences and truths of servanthood,
  worshipful emptying on a wanderer's path,
  in unity atoning by catholicity of life,
  with reverence open to the spirit . . . .

One blessed moment flashing by.

And all this hurries to the end, so fast,
  that muddled minds whizz along,
  cyclically probing: What was meant? Where to begin?
    How to live it?   How to apply?

One blessed moment passing by.

(Francis valued what Christ valued: minority, servanthood, unity, Catholicity, atonement, pilgrimage, worship and reverence. Francis' life, like Christ's was "one blessed moment passing by."   Sr. M.T.)

bROTheR JUNipeR ANd

It chanced upon a certain day
An ailing Friar was heard to say:
"Pig's foot my taste would satisfy;
I wish I had one ere I die,
But I must quell this great desire
For I'm a poor and humble Friar. Ah, me! Ah, me!"

Now Juniper, a kindly man,
Formed in his heart a noble plan;
His brother must not yearn in vain;
Pig's foot for him he must obtain.
Forth from his convent hastened he
To do a work of charity. Went he! Went he!

A neighbor's pig was quite nearby;
To cut the pig's foot he would try.
"Now little pig," he said, "stand still;
My brother lies abed, quite ill.
I do not ask you for your life;
I'll take your foot with this sharp knife!" "Oink, oink! Oink, oink!"

The Pig

The operation did succeed.
Fra Juniper had done the deed.
Elated at his charity,
To cook the pig's foot hastened he;
And as this dish he did prepare
He raised to God a thankful prayer. "Amen. Amen."

The poor pig screeched and stamped and squealed
And with his three feet kicked and reeled.
In fact, so loud a noise made he
His owner hurried out to see
How he had met this dreadful end,
The guilty one to apprehend. "Who's here? Who's here?"

A mighty anger seized his soul.
His fury was beyond control.
Then, when he saw what had been done
He swore he'd find the guilty one!
Straight to the Friary he went
To give his dreadful rage full vent. "Roar, roar! Roar, roar!"

Then Father Francis went about
The evil-doer to find out,
That he might make a recompense
For such a terrible offence,
So Juniper on bended knee,
Sought pardon with humility. "Ah, me! Ah, me!"

'Twas hard for Juniper to see
How anyone could angry be,
Since God made all things for our use;
How could a neighbor then refuse
To sacrifice one foot of four,
Since Brother Pig still had three more: "Oink, oink! Oink, oink!"

Then Juniper with gentle word,
More sweet than he had ever heard,
Convinced the man his love would gain
More than the whole pig could obtain.
So softening the owner's heart
That with the whole pig he did part. "*All's well! All's well!*"

Ah, Father Francis, did you jest
When openly you once confessed
And showed how much you did admire
This dear, unique and simple Friar;
"*I would be very, very pleased*
To have a forest of such trees!" "*Quite so! Quite so!*"

(Brother Juniper was a simple Friar. The tale related here gives evidence of his guilelessness and charity toward his brothers.   Sr. R.M.)

BROTHER JUNIPER AND THE SEE-SAW

*Fra Juniper left home
That he might visit Rome
And many came to see
This man of sanctity.
They lined the street,
The holy one to greet,
And walk with him through Rome
Straight to his convent home.
They swarmed about,
Did loudly shout.
He paid no heed,
Oh, no, indeed!
His air of unconcern
Was neither gay nor stern.*

He spied two tots at play;
Upon a see-saw they
Went gaily up and down
And minded none around.
He then went in haste,
A little one displaced
And up and down he went
In peaceful merriment.
Then to and fro
The two did go.
Some watched his play
And tried to pray.
Though some did loudly plead,
The good man paid no heed.

The people stood in awe
To watch their saint see-saw;
As up and down they went,
Some moaned in discontent;
"How sad! How sad!
He surely must be mad!"
Even those of loyal heart
Had finally to depart.
See-saw went on
Till all were gone.
Then, humbly he
Went quietly
With none to pay him heed.
Thus did his trick succeed.

�֍

(As Christ escaped from the crowd when they wished to make him King—so too—Juniper escapes from those who would revere him.   Sr. R.M.)

BROTHER FLY

Have you seen him flitting round?
Have you heard his buzzing sound?
Watch him! In and out he'll go
Back and forth and to and fro.
First he's here and then he's there,
Till you think he's everywhere.
Can you stop him? No, no, no!
Can you stop him? No, no, no!
'Tis not you; 'tis not I!
We are not that Brother Fly.

Father Francis spoke with scorn
When his children he did warn
Of the one who goes about
Bits of scandal to find out;
Let this idler pass you by,
He is just a Brother Fly
On his aimless, fruitless route.
On his aimless, fruitless route.
'Tis not you; 'tis not I!
We are not that Brother Fly.

Brother Fly is seldom seen
Through the recollection screen.
He can't pick up crumbs of news
When to gossip we refuse;
If we work and love and pray,
We can keep this pest away.
Then his power he will lose.
Then his power he will lose.
'Tis not you; 'tis not I!
We are not that Brother Fly.

(The only creature St. Francis ever complained about was the fly. He likens the lazy, gossipy Friar to a useless fly.   Sr. R.M.)

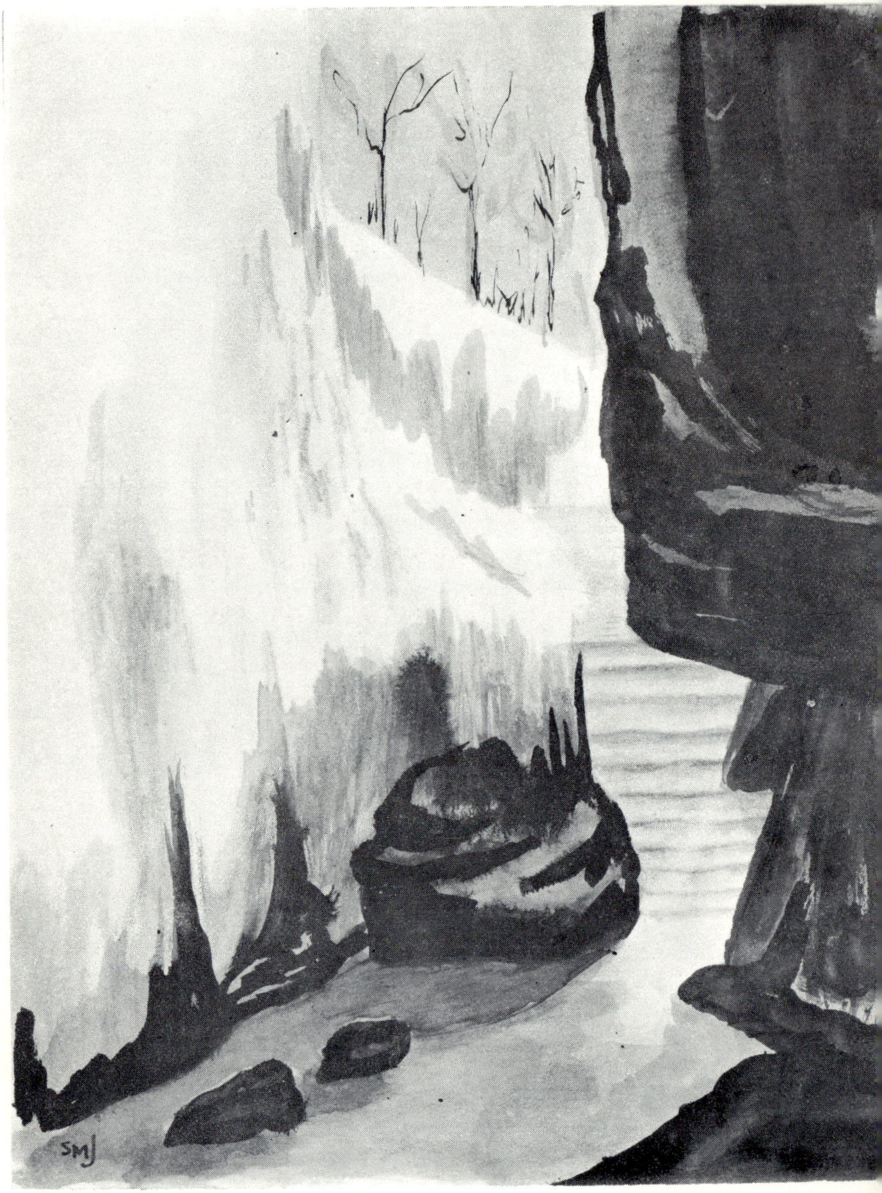
SMJ

LA VERNA

Stealthy sunlight edging
                  its way
                          around the trees
      grappling with the earth below
Stopped by massive cliffs
                  overhanging cool-shelters
      formed, so they say, by the man-God's death
To become a place for
                  reverent quietude
                          deep
                                unsurpassed
     contemplative
Yet—unaware of
            its own frightfulness
            its might
            its power

            over those who there now pray!

(It was on Mount LaVerna where St. Francis saw the vision of the six-winged Seraph and received the wounds of Christ.   Sr. M.T.)

THE BLINDNESS OF ST. FRANCIS

Your last two years were dark and filled with pain;
But never did you lose your "perfect joy."
The light of "Brother Sun" for you did wane
But nothing could your inner light destroy.

Closed were those eyes that wondrous rapture knew;
For fragrant flower, for beast and fluttering bird—
But rapture still possessed the heart of you,
And still your mind God's tender music heard:

Your hymn to joy, your canticle of praise,
Your prayer for peace, your letter to all men.
Now, by your patient, suffering ways
You witness, as you breathe your love's "Amen."

(Francis suffered with an eye disease for many years until he became totally blind. Yet—he could rejoice in what God had given him.   Sr. R.M.)

BE GENTLE, BROTHER FIRE

"Be gentle, Brother Fire;
    Don't scorch when you are near,
The one you are to cauterize
    Considers you most dear . . . .
Dear Brother Fire, be kind—
    To this, your patient, blind,
Do your work with fiery skill
    But sear not to disturb his will.

"I feel your heat; yet, reft of light.
I know you'll try to restore my sight.
Our common bond, the Lord of all,
Summoned me to heed your call.

"Oh, gently, gently, as you approach;
Upon your powers I'll not encroach!
The heat you give to warm men's homes
I pray will not destroy my bones.

"Closer yet—and once again,
Be gentle to this man of sin.
So near—so near—like rays of sun.
How now? The doctor says he's done?

"How sweet, how kind, dear fiery Brother,
Your heat, your flames, did not much bother
So that I knew not you were done,
You worked as gently as Brother Sun."

(Francis' love for creatures had given him an unusual power of command over them. While he was undergoing the painful cauterization for his eyes he begged Brother Fire to be gentle to him. And Francis, it is reported, felt no pain.   Sr. M.T.)

THE LOST RULE

"What? Lost? What a loss!
The Rule without gloss!
Some traitor hand has done this.

"Again, again, must I write a Rule?
If I must—I'll play the Lord's fool.
As he dictates words for eternal bliss.

"Poverty stands in fact and print.
No goods! No superficial stint
To while away one's time.

"No money! No means but providence,
And no excuse like giving offence
To patrons who live so fine.

"We live on God's word;
Not by the sword,
Until the day He calls.

"In mercy and love and joy and peace,
In hope and sorrow—our ranks will increase,
Helping each brother when he falls.

*"Gospel spirit and life, our Rule will be
If my followers will follow me,
By words from God's own voice.*

*"A Rule inspired by God's own Son;
We know the victory He has won,
And to live this, is a matter of choice.*

*"No! I'll not change one syllable!
God has given it! It is His will!
And I will live it personally.*

*"Those who wish it changed again
Are neither Catholic nor religious men
Destined to live eternally."*

(The primitive Rule was lost and never found. Francis resolved to write it again, for he feared that it was lost because some of the Friars did not want to live the poverty which distinguished their way of life from the other Orders.   Sr. M.T.)

hymn to saint clare

St. Clare, most valiant woman,
So eager for the palm;
From first to last a heroine,
With confidence and calm.
No wealth, no power could lure you;
Christ was your sword and shield;
They fled who came to take you,
Alone you won the field.

When Saracen's fierce army
Stood even at the gate,
You went with dauntless courage
This force to dissipate.
In your frail hands you carried
The Conqueror and King;
The army fled in terror
Like wild birds on the wing.

Yes, even in the household
A war you had to wage
When kindness led Christ's vicar
Your rigors to assuage;
But, poverty, your treasure,
No man could take away;
For Jesus gave it to you
And it was yours for aye.

Francis, himself, did clothe you
In garments, rough and poor;
And for his dear, Poor Ladies
He found a spot secure;
Our Father Francis loved you,
His daughter, young and fair;
And we, your children praise you,
Our own beloved St. Clare.

※

(Clare was the first woman to ask acceptance into the **Order**. Since women, in those days, who sought religious life, were cloistered, she founded the Second Order—cloistered nuns—but adjusted the life to the poverty which Francis had introduced for his followers.   Sr. R.M.)

The Gospel story is all he needs—
The reading fills his soul.

So Francis walks in darkest light;
And sings his song with lightest heart!

Despised, discouraged, deprived, unwanted—
In his latest hours.

The light in darkness gleams more clear
As Sister Death draws near.

"What is written is God's"—he proclaimed—
"Not a word is to be changed!"

His hands, his feet, his side, all speak
The victory that is his.

And death embraced his cheerful soul
As she smiled on her gentle guest.

Leaving his body supple and whole
White as a new-born child.

Never so beautiful in life
As the Eternal gaze now styled.

(Francis' body, which had been so frail, dark and stiffened with pain, became supple and milk-white after his death. The whole of it resembled a white marble statue with black nails in the hands and feet.   Sr. M.T.)

WATCHMAN

Gently bending branches,
Lost in the nightness of things,
Move rhythmically
As the nightingale sings.

Harmony of moving branches
Like a melody from a world unseen,
Hopefully lulling man to rest
Mesmerized in a placid dream.

Groping, swaying branches
Against a velvet-twinkling sky—
How many seasons have you announced?
How many generations have you waved by?

Younger than the citadel
That watches yonder town;
Yet, older than the dying man
Who lies upon the ground,

You, too, did watch as once he called
The birds from off your branches fair
And preached to them of peace and love
To spread this message everywhere.

Gently bending branches
Lost in the lifeness of things,
Bend lovingly toward him—
For now it is the Lark who sings.

(If dumb creatures could speak, such as the trees which grow about Assisi, one wonders what they would tell.   Sr. M.T.)

These Friendships Were Made in Heaven

St. Francis met St. Dominic in a dream—
A dream that he would find was very real;
For often 'tis a part of God's blest scheme,
One servant to another to reveal.

When in a church these two great builders met,
St. Francis, knowing he had seen that face—
The face which now he never would forget,
Greeted his brother with a warm embrace.

And is it strange that in a later time,
St. Thomas and St. Bonaventure shared
A friendship we might almost call divine,
Because, in truth, by heaven it was prepared!

I did not meet you in a vivid dream,
Yet, circumstances too, were meant to be;
We are a part of God's most loving scheme,
The heirs of our beloved family.

(St. Francis and St. Dominic were two great contemporary reformers. We are told of the great friendship that grew up between them and their orders.   Sr. R.M.)

FRANCIS BLESSES ASSISI

I bless you, fair Assisi;
Though my eyes are closed to sight,
Your rolling hills and vineyards
Remain memory's fond delight.

God grant much peace and joy
To those who dwell within
Your city's gates and walls,
And keep them free from sin.

I bless you, sweet Assisi,
With your stately citadel,
Your stony walks and narrow streets;
May the good God treat you well!

God grant my life within you
Has a fruitful harvest borne,
And all who enter in the town
Of evil will be shorn.

I bless you, kind Assisi,
As my life is nearly done,
And beg the God who loves you
To smile through Brother Sun.

(As Francis was taken from the Bishop's palace back to die at the Portiuncula, he asked to stop and be turned to face Assisi once more—so he could bless it for the last time.   Sr. M.T.)

CANTICLE TO BROTHER FRANCIS

Most High, all-powerful, good Lord!
 All praise is yours, all glory, all honor,
 And all blessings.

All praise be yours, my Lord, through all that you have made
 And first my Lord, through Brother Francis
 Who brings a rule of life; the light by which we live.

How exemplary is he, how perfect in observance!
 Of You, most High, he bears the likeness.

All praise be yours, my Lord, through Sister Clare and
 Brother Jacoba,
 In whose great care our Father rested
 When eternity was near.

All praise be yours, my Lord, through Brothers Leo and Angelo,
 Through whose great pen and voice
 This canticle was learned.

All praise be yours, my Lord, through Brother Mountain,
 LaVerna is its name,
 On whose great heights the jewels of life were given.